Dear Sasha,

Thank you for purchasing my book! being a part of my supporting me always, enjoy it, lots

Kam xxx

YOUR WAY OR THE HIGHWAY

How to Become the Director of Your Life

Kam Bedi

YOUR WAY OR THE HIGHWAY —

How to Become the Director of Your Life

Printed in the United Kingdom

Published in the United Kingdom

ISBN 13: 978-1534911796

ACKNOWLEDGEMENTS

I'd like to take this opportunity to thank first and foremost the universe and God for guiding me through this amazing experience. Despite my ups and downs I have been shown the signs of how to get through my writing while dealing with continuous disruptions and obstacles.

I also want to thank my family, who have been patient towards my lack of presence in their lives and who have been so supportive through my book writing journey. If it wasn't for their understanding, I may have struggled!

A big thank you to my friends (you know who you are) for putting up with my 'down days' and my frustrations. They are the people I always turn to and in return their encouragement and support has made a huge impact in my life to date.

Lastly a big thank you to Tunji Ogunjimi, my book coach for his encouragement, support and understanding through my journey. I am truly honoured and forever grateful for having the opportunity to work with you.

CONTENTS PAGE

INTRODUCTION

First of all I'd like to thank you for purchasing this book and wanting to find out more about it. My guess is that you have acquired this book because you want to make some massive changes in your life and yes of course, you have probably already read numerous personal development books and are right now thinking 'how is this any different?' Or maybe this is your first personal development book. In that case I feel honoured and privileged, and hope that you take something away from reading it, even if it's just one thing. Just to give you a brief idea of what to expect, I will talk about some major issues people experience when creating their own destiny. I will share with you some useful tips and strategies to help you move forward. I have used them and have been successful in moving forward. This book will not cover every aspect of life and talk about setting goals and taking action in detail, but rather recommend how to start creating the 'real' you and the life you want through some easy to follow steps.

Maybe you're going through something life changing at the moment, it could be something difficult or it could be a positive change, maybe you don't even what it is and how you actually feel but I'm here to tell you that it's ok as I've been there.

Let me start by asking you a few questions, please take at least ten minutes to write your answers on a piece of paper. Once you have answered the questions display your answers somewhere where you can see them every day.

1. Do you know what your purpose is in life?
2. What makes you happy?
3. What do you *really* want for yourself in life?

Before we even think about helping others or help change the world we must start from within. I would suggest starting with your mindset.

Chapter 1. MINDSET

POSITIVE THINKING

This idea can sound a bit soft and fluffy, which is something of a problem for many people who recognise that thinking good thoughts won't change the world and therefore discard the whole idea, however I see positive thinking as a way of taking the negative experiences or situations presented to me as 'lessons learnt.' I'm sure you've been through some really tough times in your life, where you have felt as though your soul has taken a beating but think of it like this, if you hadn't got through what you did, would you be reading this now?

The point I'm trying to make is at the time you didn't realise it but you *did* get through it, because you are still alive. In every negative situation there's a positive turnaround, so rather than realising it months or years down the line why not acknowledge it, accept it and take steps to move forward. More often than not, 'negative experiences' are actually 'lessons to be learnt,' which occur to help you in the future. I was never a positive person, I complained and moaned about everything in life, if you saw my face a few years back you'd want to slap me! Nothing improved; the more negative I was, the unhappier I became and the less satisfied in life...you see where I'm going with this.

Here are a few ways to get that positivity back into your life or to introduce it:

Have a Positive Support Group

It's important to have a positive support group to help each other through difficult times. Notice I said a "positive" support group. Surrounding yourself with positive people will help you stay positive when in a negative situation. There are plenty of negative people out there — avoid them! Their negative attitudes will only bring you down and be counterproductive to what you are trying to achieve by practicing positive thinking.

Express What You Are Grateful for

I cannot stress this enough! Even in the worst of times, most of us realize that we still have things in our lives for which we can be grateful. Voice those blessings! Practice gratitude. Talk about the things you are grateful for with your closest friends, your support group. Keep a gratitude journal to capture the thankfulness you feel for what you have on a daily basis. Actively acknowledging what you're grateful for will help you to always have a grateful mind and heart, even when negative things happen, but also remember to feel what you're saying. Don't just say it, mean it with all your heart.

Exercise Your Body and Mind

We know that exercise is good for our bodies, but what about our minds? Sure, it is! It releases those natural endorphins in our brains that make us feel better. Exercise has physical as well as mental and emotional benefits. Getting out there and moving around will keep your body in better shape, as well as boosting your self-esteem for having the discipline to exercise. You might try adding yoga into your regime now and then to help you learn to really focus and meditate. Exercise is an excellent way to fight the negative effects of bad situations

Accept and Find Solutions

Many of us are resistant to change in our lives. What we must do is learn to accept that change *will* happen. Haven't you heard that "the only constant in life is change"? There is a lot of truth to that, as we continually go through changes, both good and bad. Accepting that changes are a part of life can help us to relax and be more accepting. For example, if you're in a bad job situation, what do you do? Accept it and try to make it better? Possibly, or maybe this is the chance to make that change and pursue that exciting job or career path you really want.

Tragic incidents, such as death, will throw us off even worse, but when our brains are practiced on how to stay positive in negative situations, even tragedy won't destroy us. With the power of positive thinking, we can learn to put negative situations in perspective and to deal with them as they arise. My motto is: Acknowledge it, Accept it, Feel it and then Move Forward.

You can start to see that just by implementing a few simple steps will help you on the road to becoming a better you and I am guessing that you really do want to, so stick at it, train your brain every day, and not just when difficult situations arise.

"You cannot tailor-make the situations in life but you can tailor-make the attitudes to fit those situations." — Zig Ziglar

BEING PRESENT

I will put my hand up and confess that I have rarely remained 'in the present' moment. You may think well I don't have to, however what people don't realise is that giving yourself that minute or two can make a huge difference between being unproductive and productive! Staying present has always been a struggle for me (it's one of the reasons I decided to write about the 'Present Moment' but I know how important it is in living a positive life. When I experience those rare moments of being fully present, I feel more centred, more positive, more creative, less stressed, less unhappy, and less frustrated. As difficult as it can be sometimes, I truly believe that being in the moment is worth every ounce of effort because it really does lead to being more positive and productive, not to mention leading you to make good decisions! Here are some of the basics things you can do to help you stay in the present moment:

Pay Attention to Thoughts

Thoughts can become so clear and certain that they seem like fact even when they are about things that haven't happened yet. When I realize what I'm thinking, and how present-minded it is, I can often direct my attention back to the now. The trick is to pay attention to your thoughts, to realize that they're just that, thoughts. They aren't necessarily facts and the more you are aware of them, the more likely you are to rule out thoughts of the past or future and stay focused on the present

Feed the Five Senses

I often think about focusing on the five senses because I've found them to be one of the best tools we have to bring us back to the now. When I find my mind wandering shamelessly into future or past territory (and I'm aware that it's happening!), I use my five senses to bring me back to the present. Instead of allowing myself to be governed by my thoughts, I take control of my thinking and ask myself, "What do you hear, taste, feel, see and smell?" Doing this takes me away from any kind of distraction and reminds me that what matters most is what's happening right at this precise moment.

Step Outside Yourself

One of the reasons I used to find myself worrying a lot is because I was often focused on me. While this isn't necessarily a bad thing, too much focus on one's self can lead to a lot of over thinking, worrying, and yes that dreaded 'S' word stress! Sound familiar? A great way to avoid this is to find others to focus on. I've found that volunteering my time to help others (or even simply asking someone else how his or her day is going and really listening to the answer) helps to take my mind away from the past or future and brings me back into the moment. If you're not with other people at the time, you can do this simply by thinking (positively) about someone else.

Write It Down (All of It!)

Sometimes one of the best ways to get out of your own head is to put all of the stuff that's in there down on paper. It might seem counter-intuitive to spend time writing about the past or future when one's trying to stay present, but I've found that when I write things down, it's often like cleaning out the closet of my mind, getting rid of all the thoughts that don't fit in there anymore. In addition to putting thoughts down on paper, writing about the present moment (and what those five senses are showing me) can be a great get-back-to-the-now exercise.

Create a Reminder

Being present can be really difficult and sometimes I need a little (or big) nudge to remind myself to stay in the moment. I've created all kinds of reminders: sticky notes, alarms on my phone, etc. and all of them have proved very useful when it comes to remembering to stay in the moment. I've given up the notion that I'll someday be one of those people that just stay present and have given in to the idea that I might always need a little reminder. Creating these is simple enough and it's so helpful when it comes to staying on track. What reminders are you going to set yourself? Do this now!

"Realize deeply that the present moment is all you ever have." — Eckhart Tolle

BELIEFS

What causes someone to persist when another would give up? What causes a person to focus and utilize all their resources towards a goal? What ultimately creates the difference between happiness and despair? The answer is beliefs.

I've tried a lot of crazy methods to improve my beliefs' structure. Most of them didn't work very well. Some of them were complete rubbish, but in trying and failing to change my beliefs with all these methods, I slowly found the right system for changing my beliefs. Changing beliefs isn't easy. Despite what some authors and speakers tell you, deeply ingrained beliefs aren't going to disappear with one magical technique or method, but if your happiness and success is important to you it can be done.

Hunt Them down

There are many ways that you can begin the process of finding damaging beliefs. For me the best way has always been reading and listening to material from successful people in that field. One of the greatest benefits of personal development content is that you subtly pick up on the belief structure of the person who is delivering it.

An even better way is to start associating with people that hold the beliefs you want. They may be difficult to find if the level of success you are seeking is rare, but if you do, their belief structure will begin to point out flaws in your own.

Often fear can keep you from finding negative beliefs. If you believe that you are unworthy of a relationship, this belief may be hard to get rid of. Why? Because then you would have to admit that for all the time in the past you could have been in a relationship if it wasn't for such a stupid belief.

Let go. The past is the past, move to the now and find those beliefs that are holding you back.

Suspend Judgment

Every time you criticize yourself for that old belief you make it stronger, because you weaken your connection to one of your greatest assets: self-compassion. Instead, access kindness, humanity, and mindfulness to create an internal support system built on acceptance, appreciation, and optimism. Forgiveness too, can be a key element in this step. I've had to focus on forgiving myself for that long-ago "failure" and shift my attention to what I can only describe as transcendence. When I approach a problem now, a part of me rises above the moment, forgives those old doubts, accepts and appreciates my apprehension, and yet believes I can easily arrive at the solution. It's this strong, calm, and peaceful part that proceeds to obtain the solution.

Uncertainty

Doubt begins to destroy beliefs. The first step in any effort to restructure your belief system must always begin here. If you don't have any doubt in a belief, you can't see it. You probably contain many empowering and damaging beliefs that you aren't even aware of because you have no doubt in them.

If you are trying to rid yourself of a negative belief, then you already have a fair bit of doubt. The next step is to intensify that doubt to a point where the belief seems almost ridiculous, because building doubt is the easiest step in this entire process, creating as much as possible is a good idea.

Let's say your belief is that you aren't attractive. You can start building doubt by finding all the moments in your life where this hasn't been true. Chances are you can summon up moments in your life when people were interested in what you had to say or gave you a compliment.

The process of building doubt shouldn't be used to procrastinate over the next step. Building doubt doesn't take long. Some beliefs will quickly look ridiculous and others you may still hold on to strongly when you need to move on. If you are struggling to build doubt then you need to just move on to the next step of testing.

Test It

Have you ever had a belief that you knew was wrong but it still influenced your behaviour? That happens when you build enough doubt consciously but your subconscious is still in favor of the old belief. The subconscious almost always wins in the battle of any behavior, so unless you can focus your willpower for the rest of your life, you need to convince the subconscious it is wrong.

To change the subconscious version of the belief you need to go out and actually test it. This is the difficult part. The subconscious mind doesn't like it when you try to do things it believes are negative. It will likely fill you with fear at the thought of challenging it. Overcoming this internal urge can be very difficult.

The best way to tackle this problem is to do as much as you can. If you are too afraid to test out the full version of your belief, try a smaller version. As your belief starts to crumble you can go further and further until it is completely removed.

This process takes time and it is the reason that changing your beliefs isn't immediate. Confidence, courage and charisma can take a long time to build because the beliefs that prevent them take time to be demolished and new ones need to be formed in their place. Systematically pushing your belief structure will slowly remove them from your subconscious.

I'm not suggesting that you shouldn't try to test as much of your belief at once if you can, but sometimes people find they can't test their belief all at once so they don't break it down and test pieces of it. The larger the chunks you can test at once, the faster the belief will be destroyed. But if you can't take down a chunk, break it up and try again.

The process for improving your beliefs, finding, doubting then testing, may sound simple or crude, but it works. Shifting your beliefs to a more empowering state can be one of the most rewarding things you will ever do. Take the time to do it properly and begin right now.

Shift from Expectation to Intention

An expectation is a strong belief that something will happen in the future. When circumstances beyond your control interfere with success, it's easy to experience a setback. An intention, however, is how you plan to approach a task or experience. This is always within your control, which means it offers more solid ground on which to build your desire for change. I really love this step because it's helped me eliminate the expectation that I'll make a mistake. Now I focus on how I intend to create a successful approach to solving the problem.

"A belief system is nothing more than a thought you've thought over and over again." — Wayne Dyer

LEARN TO SAY NO!

I understand that we want everyone to be happy and to please people, those people are called 'People Pleasers' I have been a serial people pleaser for years now and only up until the last couple of years have I realized that it can and will backfire on you at some point in the future. I could tell you to just cut it out but I know it's easier said than done, so here is some useful advice on how to stop people pleasing and learning to say no.

Don't Wait until You're Fed up

Whether it's spouse, family member or friend, when you hold onto your feelings, you're eventually going to explode. You can ignore little things but if the person has really upset you or their actions grate on you by doing the same things repeatedly, don't let ill feelings fester too long. Initiate a discussion about the problem when you're calm and before you've built up resentment.

Don't Feel Guilty. You Can't Say YES to Everything

Even the best of friends don't always agree or see things eye to eye. Your friend may think it's perfectly reasonable to ask a favour of you but you may feel otherwise. True friends have to be sensitive to each other's feelings and be willing to accept NO for an answer when it's reasonable. Of course, we all want to help out our friends and support them but if the personal cost of saying yes is too great, either morally or logistically, it's okay to say NO!

If your friend can't accept NO for an answer, recognize it as his/her problem not yours. Some people are extremely self-centred and demanding, to the point of taking their friends (and others) for granted. Your friend may be overwhelmed by problems or just totally wrapped up in him/her self. This person may have a hard time accepting NO under any circumstances, particularly if they are accustomed to hearing you say yes. In this case, you need to be firm and not back down.

Try to Say NO as Graciously as You Can

Saying NO doesn't have to sound harsh and can actually be couched in some tender terms to help soften the blow. You might say, "I wish I could but" or "I really can't because..." Providing a reasonable explanation of why you're saying NO always helps the other person understand your decision, having said that I would say it depends on the nature of the relationship, you therefore do not always need to justify your reasons.

If you are unable to say NO, even when you want to, find out what's holding you back. Some people are unable to say NO because their need to be liked is great and their self-confidence is lacking. If you have this problem and it's interfering with your relationships-personal or professional-you may want to speak to a coach, who can help you better understand the problem and address it.

Know the Implications of Saying YES

We normally say yes to the little requests streaming in because it may seem like a small deal. Just chip in and help if we can — what's the problem? It doesn't take much time, maybe just ten to fifteen minutes, or twenty minutes max. Right?

Yet, these little moments pile up over time to become big chunks of time. There's a reason why top executives, despite managing large companies and businesses, can have time for themselves, their families, friends and work all the time, while some people who are always busy day-in and day-out and yet never seem to progress in their life situations. It's as if the latter group is busy running to stay in the same spot. That's because the former knows the implications of not saying no.

Whenever you get a request, think twice before you say yes or no. What's going to happen if you say yes to it? What are the long-term implications? What is there to gain? What are you going to lose if you agree? Do you really have to say yes? What limiting beliefs do you have that are making you say yes?

I believe that time is more precious than money, because while you can earn back money, you can never get back time. Because of that, I really value my time — it's my most precious commodity and I'm very conscious of how I spend it. You should too.

"When you say 'No' to someone, don't spend too much time justifying yourself because when you do, you lose self-control." — Kam Bedi

Chapter 2. IDENTITY

Who you are is your-self-identity, the way you look at yourself and your relationship to the world. Understanding this, allows you to examine who you are and more importantly create who you want to be, it can mean a number of things such as, the way you look, the way you talk, your beliefs and values, your confidence level and even your body posture.

It's important to take time out to really get to know you and spend some time with yourself. It might sound a bit daft but believe me it isn't if you really think about it. I'll give you an example of this, a few years ago, I was in such a dark place (as a result of many negative experiences in my life) mainly personal, I didn't even know how to come across, speak or behave or even what I really wanted in life. I did not even know the importance of self-love; I thought the concept of self-love was being big headed! It took me a long time to gain self-discovery which involved a lot of things as I'll talk about now.

LACK OF CONFIDENCE

It's important to understand that confidence can come and go. If you feel that your confidence has taken a knock — that's fine. There are things that you can do to build it up again. If you feel overwhelmed or uncertain, that's fine too. There is always a way forward.

You may be confident generally, but find in certain situations that you 'wobble'. Or it may be that you have always lacked confidence in yourself and your own abilities. You may not even like yourself very much, although this may be due to low self-esteem. Here are some ways of building up your confidence or to re-gain it from a knock back.

Self-confidence allows you to have positive yet realistic views of yourself and the situations in which you are involved. If you have self-confidence, typically you do not fear challenges, you are able to stand up for what you believe, and you have the courage to admit your limitations.

Most of us have areas in our lives where we feel quite competent while at the same recognizing areas where we do not feel at all confident. Having an accurate sense of self-confidence means you avoid behaving in an overconfident or reckless way. It means you are not afraid to take risks on tasks that you are able to do and you do not get paralyzed by the fear and anxiety when faced with things you want or need to do. Have a look at the tips below for building self-confidence:

Develop Awareness

When we're aware, we can recognize how we are responding and reacting to our own fears, creating a moment between our emotions and our actions. We can then choose to respond in a healthier way and it's about choice; you become what you *choose* to believe about yourself.

Write in a Journal

Many of our thoughts and feelings are locked in our subconscious mind and writing can help to bring them into our awareness. Writing about the way we feel and think can help to separate negative ideas about ourselves from who we really are; it is also a healthy way of releasing any tension or negativity that's built up inside you.

I personally recommend doing this, you could even write about your thoughts (and if appropriate to the situation) then bin/burn the paper, not only does this give you a sense of relief but also closure to certain situations you'd like to resolve 'in your mind'.

Develop a Beginner's Mind

The beginner's mind is a wonderful strategy that can help us to learn all this stuff; mysticism, spirituality and metaphysics much more easily. The idea behind this strategy is that you take all of the things you know, all your brilliant opinions, all your reason and logic, even your cherished beliefs and you put all this stuff on the shelf for a while. (Now, please note, it will all still be there safe and sound when you get back!)

When you have a beginner's mind, you look at things as if you are seeing them for the first time, with openness, eagerness and freedom from expectation. You can see things in a new light, rather than automatically responding with the same old patterns of behaviour. This isn't easy to do especially when you have been conditioned to think a certain way, but through practise every day it does become easier.

Let Go

I could write a whole book about how I should be, what I should have done and what I should be doing, couldn't you? The world seems to be full of experts on my life who like to tell me what I should be doing. Living with a beginner's mind means letting go of those *shoulds.* I'm not advocating living without moral standards. I think that most of our 'shoulds' reflect other peoples' ideas on what our life should look like. We can let go of them.

Non-attachment, or letting go, is the goal of mindfulness. When you let go of what you think you should do or who you should be, you can trust yourself and choose what's right for you, it's not as easy as it sounds, however it is possible, you just need to tell your mind that!

"With confidence you have won, before you have started." — Marcus Garvey

VALUES

Your values are the things that you believe are important in the way you live and work. They (should) determine your priorities and, deep down, they're probably the measures you use to tell if your life is turning out the way you want it to.

When the things that you do and the way you behave match your values, life is usually good — you're satisfied and content, but when these don't align with your personal values that's when things feel wrong. This can be a real source of unhappiness.

Values exist, whether you recognize them or not. Life can be much easier when you acknowledge your values — and when you make plans and decisions that honour them. If you value family, but you have to work a seventy-hour week in your job, will you feel internal stress and conflict? And if you don't value competition, and you work in a highly competitive sales environment, are you likely to be satisfied with your job?

In these types of situation, understanding your values can really help. When you know your own values, you can use them to make decisions about how to live your life.

When you define your personal values, you discover what's truly important to you. A good way of starting to do this is to look back on your life — to identify when you felt really good, and really confident that you were making good choices.

These are some of the ways you can answer to help you identify values or revalue them:

Determine Your Top Values, Based on Your Experiences of Happiness, Pride, and Fulfilment

Values are usually fairly stable, yet they don't have strict limits or boundaries. Also, as you move through life, your values may change. For example, when you start your career, success measured by money and status might be a top priority. But after you have a family, work-life balance may be what you value more.

As your definition of success changes, so do your personal values. This is why keeping in touch with your values is a lifelong exercise. You should continuously revisit this, especially if you start to feel unbalanced... and you can't quite figure out why.

Prioritize Your Top Values

This is when you must know which value is more important to you. Write down your top values, not in any particular order.

Look at the first two values and ask yourself, "If I could satisfy only one of these, which would I choose?" It might help to visualize a situation in which you would have to make that choice.

Keep working through the list, by comparing each value with each other value, until your list is in the correct order.

Reaffirm Your Values

Check your top-priority values, and make sure they fit with your life and your vision for yourself.

Do these values make you feel good about yourself? Are you proud of your top three values? Would you be comfortable and proud to tell your values to people you respect and admire? Do these values represent things you would support, even if your choice isn't popular, and it puts you in the minority?

When you consider your values in decision making, you can be sure to keep your sense of integrity and what you know is right, and approach decisions with confidence and clarity. You'll also know that what you're doing is best for your current and future happiness and satisfaction. Making value-based choices may not always be easy. However, making a choice that you know is right is a lot less difficult in the long run.

Identifying and understanding your values is a challenging and important exercise. Your personal values are a central part of who you are — and who you want to be. By becoming more aware of these important factors in your life, you can use them as a guide to make the best choice in any situation. Some of life's decisions are really about determining what you value most. When many options seem reasonable, it's helpful and comforting to rely on your values — and use them as a strong guiding force to point you in the right direction.

"Open your arms to change, but don't let go of your values." — Dalai Lama

LACK OF EXPRESSION

This concept has always been something I have struggled with — why? Because I was always so timid and shy and didn't have the confidence, I wasn't the popular one at school I was not noticed by any of the boys in school/college (poor me)! More importantly when life hit me with some difficult truths, I soon realized I had to make some serious changes. Here are some of the tips I have followed but have not limited myself to, in order to help me express myself freely.

Yes, it's scary to put yourself out there and to have people judge you. But if you know who you are and what you stand for, does it matter what others think, when you know the truth and what it means to you.

Stand for Something

This is important. It allows you to let your personality shine. It is also the foundation of your values, which help shape your identity, allowing people to connect with you, enabling you to surround yourself with like-minded people for support.

Remember, no man is an island, as John Donne wrote: "We, as human beings, need to interact with another and need each other to find fulfillment in our lives" So stand for something to build your world of lovers and 'haters,' instead of having no supporters or challengers to help you grow.

Let Go of the Outcome

Sometimes we say things or do things because we want to get a certain reaction or action out of people however, keeping in mind we have no control over anything in life (except for our actions and our responses) why not speak your truth anyway?

Your body and mind will be grateful because you are being honest with yourself. In the end, whatever happens, you've got nothing to lose because you have honored your truth. No regrets.

Set an Example

The best way to stand up for a belief is to walk the walk, not just talk the talk. If you really believe in something, then don't just argue, do something about it. Attend fundraisers for awareness, get involved locally, and get yourself out there. Say what you mean and mean what you say, I'm a firm believer in making sure my words match my actions. The bonus here is if you're willing to put in the extra effort, then you know it really means something to you.

You Only Need to Impress Yourself

Yes, it's scary to put yourself out there to have people judge you. But if you know who you are and what you stand for, does it matter what others think, when you know your truth and what it means to you?

The truth is that, if you are comfortable in your own skin, what others think of you probably won't bother you that much. After all, you will always have people who will be for you or against you, so why not stand for something and just be you? What's the worst thing that could happen?

"In the end people will judge you anyway, so don't live your life impressing others. Live your life impressing yourself." — Kam Bedi

SELF-LOVE/SELF WORTH

Self-love is a popular term today that gets tossed around in normal conversation. "You have to love yourself more." "Why don't you love yourself?" "If you only loved yourself, this wouldn't have happened to you." "You can't love another person until you love yourself first." These are just a few of the self-love directives that we give or get to suggest a way to achieving more fulfilment.

Self-love is important to living well. It influences who you pick for a mate, the image you project at work, and how you cope with the problems in your life. It is so important to your welfare that I want you to know how to bring more of it into your life.

I would sum up the definition of self-love as, choosing ourselves, even if it means upsetting others, of course not intentionally and not to make ourselves unpopular. Telling what is true for us, not swallowing words that express what we truly feel, think, or want to do, for example, leaving a party before anyone else because you feel tired, overwhelmed, or just plain feel done with the crowd. These are some of the ways in which I learnt the concept of self-love, which I hope you feel are useful.

Show Compassion toward Yourself

We love to beat ourselves up, you've done it, I've done it but does it help or serve you? — Not at all! You deserve love as much as anyone else. Self-compassion simply means providing yourself with the love, safety and acceptance you need to be happy!

Focus on the Things You Like about Yourself

We have a tendency to focus on the things we don't like about ourselves: our flaws, insecurities, mistakes or fears. However, the more you focus on what you don't like about yourself, the more those thoughts grow and turn into beliefs and start to shape your reality. Everything you perceive in the physical world has its origin in the invisible, inner world of your thoughts, beliefs and stories. When you choose to focus on yourself in a positive, compassionate way, you open yourself to seeing and realizing how amazing you already are. Take a couple minutes right now to think about the positive things about yourself, and to write down three things in your journal or on a sticky note.

Let Go of Mistakes and Embrace the Past

Imagine walking through life with a heavy backpack full of rocks. Often, our past mistakes and struggles can weigh us down, therefore preventing us from living in the moment and making the changes necessary to create an authentic life. The truth is, we all have a past and we've all made mistakes — some big, some small. But by holding on to what happened yesterday, you miss out on the beauty of the present moment, which we talked about earlier on.

Remember that everything that happened to you has shaped you into the unique person you are today, but doesn't define your future. When you embrace the past you create space for all the beautiful things the word has to offer and you open your heart to healing, love, and happiness.

Appreciate Your Life

We have a tendency to focus on the things we want to change about ourselves, our relationships and our lives. But what if you stopped focusing on the things you want to change and, instead, focused on the things you are grateful for right now. Rhonda Byrne, producer and author of The Magic, encourages us to count our blessings and be grateful for what we have.

I highly recommend this book as it did help change my life. I am a strong believer that it is a collective of many of my experiences and use of resources that have helped changed my life not just one thing.

When you train your mind to appreciate yourself and embrace all the things you're grateful for in your life you will immediately start loving yourself more. What are the things you are grateful for in your life right now? Write out the first 5 things that come to your mind and keep them somewhere where you can refer to them.

"The most terrifying thing is to accept oneself complexly." — Carl Jung

Chapter 3. PASSION

What does passionate mean? Often when I ask people this question they look at me with a confused expression on their face. The reason for this is because society has become so robotic, we wake up, go to work, come home and start that cycle again for the next day and it's no wonder we are not feeling happy or fulfilled!

BEING PASSIONATE

I've always worked hard at whatever I've been doing. My work-ethic comes from doing what I enjoy, and not forcing myself to do something. Highly passionate people aren't just lucky, they share common characteristics. They work hard, they trust their intuition and they persevere.

I don't see myself having any other option other than following my passion. Without following my purpose, life would be without color, joy and meaning. We all have the necessary abilities; we just need to let them shine.

In order to be passionate you need to find that thing that makes you want to jump up before your alarm and not see work as 'work' but something you love doing. Here are some ways for you incorporate being more passionate in your life.

Learn Everything You Can about Your Passion

If you really want to be passionate, then you have to be determined to learn everything there is to know about your passion and to continue to gain knowledge and know that there is always more to learn. Read all of the books, articles, and material that you can, take classes, read interviews, and do whatever you can to really feel like you have an understanding of what it means to succeed in your passion.

Get Advice and Insight from Other People in Your Field

Though you can learn a lot from reading or watching videos, there's something to be said for getting more hands-on information from people who know their stuff. Whether you're talking to an expert in your field or another person who shares your passion, you can always get more advice, insight, and a fresh perspective from the people around you. Don't ever think you have all of the answers and always make an effort to hear others out.

Set Goals and Meet Them

If you want to really be passionate, then you have to have a plan. Though you may think of passion as this crazy, wild, unbridled thing that can't be curbed, if you're really serious about carrying it through, then you should have a plan for how to succeed in realizing your dreams and furthering your passion. Create a series of little goals that lead up to a larger goal so you feel motivated to succeed along the way.

Be Selective

I used to have a problem with jumping into too many things at once. I think we all have many interests, which is a good thing, but it's a double-edged sword. We want to do everything at once. Often when I ask someone what they want to do, they rabble up a dozen different things. What works for me is relentless focus. I pick one thing, maybe two, and focus on them until I feel like it's time to move on. How do I pick? I notice what I resonate with, and what feels magnetic. For some, this may seem irresponsible, but to me, it's the most responsible thing I can do. When you try and tackle many things at once, more often than not, you don't finish any of the projects to your intended level of satisfaction.

Prioritization

Prioritization goes hand in hand with being selective. I know people that don't have time, and I know people that make time. It's not that you don't have enough time; it's that you fail to prioritize.

I've received a lot of e-mails and calls about time management issues. I know some people are single-mothers, working two jobs while juggling two kids. I have no idea how tough that is, but I do know that if you really want something, there are ways to make time and prioritize, even if it starts with a few minutes per day. No matter how tough your situation is, you can always do something. Don't worry about reaching your goal, just worry about making today more fulfilling than yesterday.

"Find something you're passionate about and keep tremendously interested in it." — Julia Child

HAPPINESS

What is happiness? What does it mean to you? Take one minute to write the answer down. Yes I do tend to throw in questions to get you thinking! Happiness can mean different things to different people, it could be that having lots of money makes you happy, it could going out with friends, or travelling abroad or being in good health, but what if you have all the above and you're still not happy, well you see I've been there. I've been in a place where I've had all of the above and still felt unhappy.

It wasn't the case of me being ungrateful I just didn't feel fulfilled and there you have it — fulfilment! We tend to say things like 'I'll be happy when I have this/do this' so when this happens in a few months, or even years' time, you still remain unhappy — fancy that, a possible lifetime of unhappiness?

It's easier said than done I know, but why not try and really figure out why you're still unhappy? There are several ways to find those triggers or as I like to call 'habits' as to why you fail to remain happy. Maybe try and look at these pointers.

Giving

Do things for others, as the more you give, the happier and fulfilled you feel. This can be done in many ways, through charity work, volunteering at your local community or simply making someone's day by smiling at them or helping them with something. The kind act is so powerful that no amount of money or fortunate came come close, try it as least once a day for a full week do something for someone else, without the expectation of receiving anything back.

Relating

Connect with people, whether it's your family or friends or even people outside of that 'circle'. Many find it difficult to connect with loved ones, it sounds crazy but in some cases it's often true. In other words, branch out by attending classes or courses for particular interests and where you'll meet 'like-minded' people who you can relate to and build strong relationships with. Not only do you widen your circle but also you gain more confidence and can end up learning so much about yourself.

So go ahead take that leap, look into local classes/community centres where you can get involved. I have found meet — up sessions to be very good for meeting people who have similar interests: www.meet.com

Exercising

Take care of your body, for some people I know this is not something you give importance to or even want to do. For those that do love exercise please continue! For those that don't like it, well let me explain something. It's not just about losing weight but can also help improve your mood. A workout at the gym or a brisk 30-minute walk can help or even if you want to get the music turned on and dance away, I cannot think of a more fun activity!

As you may already know physical activity stimulates various brain chemicals that may leave you feeling happier and more relaxed. You may also feel better about your appearance and yourself when you exercise regularly, which can boost your confidence and improve your self-esteem.

Acceptance

Be comfortable with who you are, no-one's perfect, but so often we compare our insides to other people's outsides. Dwelling on our flaws — what we're not rather than what we've got — makes it much harder to be happy. Learning to accept ourselves, flaws and all, and being kinder to ourselves when things go wrong, increases our enjoyment of life, our resilience and our well-being.

Having constant criticism in our heads about not being good enough is a sure way to be unhappy. This doesn't mean we should ignore our weaker areas or bad stuff that happens, but it does mean accepting that no-one is perfect. It means putting our imperfections (and things that happen to us) into perspective — seeing them as normal rather than out of the ordinary and it means a shift of focus, from what we don't have or can't do to what we have or can do.

"Be happy with what you have. Be excited about what you want." — Alan Cohen

POTENTIAL

Are you reaching your full potential or are you 'just getting by'? Do you want to reach your potential as you think about the kind of life you really want? I know for one, that for a very long time I'd just done this, or just done without thinking about whether I can do a whole lot more, until I actually did more. I realised over time I could do more and more — there was no limit! Here are some things you can look into to really reach your full potential:

Start from Within

To reach your full potential, you have to first have a better idea of what your potentials are. You have to know who you really are, what you've accomplished in the past, and what you failed to do. Be aware of what you're doing now and what you can still do in the future. Allow yourself more quiet time, spent alone, Don't hesitate to take a break from your work or business for a while. Find time for self-reflection or meditation to clear your mind, purify your heart, and lighten up your soul!

Know the End

Knowing the ultimate you is pivotal to reaching your full potential. You have to ask questions, such as what do you want people to remember about you when you die or what legacy do you want to leave with humanity when you're gone from this world? Many people are afraid to even think of their death, and this can hinder them in realizing their greatness. If you want to reach your ultimate potential, understand your final life. It is only by acknowledging your current life that you can discover your ultimate strengths and powers.

Make a Choice

Hopping from one journey to another will not help you have a longer, deeper and greater journey. To reach your full potential, you have to make a choice of what journey you will complete for the rest of your life. If you already know your end, travel the journey or related journeys to reach that destination. Make a choice and stick to it so you won't be wasting time, money and energy in travelling those journeys that don't relate to your ultimate destination.

Take Baby Steps

Action fights doubts. By taking small steps each day, you're building evidence to show your mind that you are greater and can do greater things than you thought.

Now that you have something to aim for, brainstorm for ways to get yourself to where you want to be. A good plan is to look to people who have already done what you'd like to do. Seek them out and learn from them. You can find out whether they have blog, coaching programs, or books that you can read. Having a mentor will help you accelerate your growth progress. They can help point out what you need to do and avoid following in their footsteps.

"Unless you try to do something beyond what you have already mastered, you will never grow." — Ralph Waldo Emerson

INTERESTS

So do you know what your interests are? If not, yes you guessed it, write down a list of everything that makes you happy. Take two minutes then stop and read through that list. I will take a wild guess here but this list is not just about things you have done recently but going back to when you were young or even a child! It could be something you did once or twice many moons ago and it's come back to you. Here are a few ways to get cracking on working on your interests.

Remember what You Loved as a Child

Often, our truest passions emerge in childhood, only to be squelched by real life pressures. So think about what you loved long before you had to worry about your career. Writing? Science experiments? Taking care of people? Getting back in touch with those instincts is an important step in finding your passion.

Eliminate Money from the Equation

If money were no object, what would you do? Would you travel? Spend all of your time with your children? Would you start a charitable organization to help abused women? Of course money can't be ignored, but don't let financial pressures dictate your choices. Your career should ultimately lead to financial freedom, but if financial freedom is the defining motivator, it's unlikely you'll end up doing what you love.

Think of What You Enjoy that You also Do Well

Focus on the things that you both enjoy and do well — whether you have a way with animals, make a killer lemon cheesecake, or are crazy for origami — and write them down. Then, narrow the list to the top three or four things. Keep it handy, review it often, and use it as your jumping-off point when you're plotting your career move.

Focus on Fun

Too often we get wrapped up in the expectations we set for ourselves. We focus on the details and the to-do lists instead of what is most important. What do you love to do? What makes you smile? If money were limitless, what would you be doing today? I've also been guilty in the past where I spent over ten years in admin and it definitely wasn't fun I can tell you. I was experienced in different roles within admin but deep down inside I knew this environment wasn't for me. If you're in this situation now, I'd suggest making some changes soon, because before you know it you'll be 'stuck' in that position for a very long time.

"Love what you do, do what you love." — Ray Bradley

SELF-DEVELOPMENT

I'm going to take a guess that you know little about self-development. What does it mean? Self-development is also known as personal-development or personal growth. It involves the growth and enhancement of all aspects of the person, the feelings the person has about himself or herself, and their effectiveness at living. It includes the development of positive life skills and the development of a realistic and healthy self-esteem.

Be Kind to Yourself

If you had a friend who spoke to you in the same way that you sometimes speak to yourself, how long would you allow that person to be your friend? The way you treat yourself sets the standard for others. You must love who you are or no one else will.

Embrace Problems

Part of living and growing up is experiencing unexpected troubles in life. People lose jobs, get sick, and sometimes die in car accidents. When you are younger, and things are going pretty well, this harsh reality can be hard to visualize. The smartest, and oftentimes hardest, thing we can do in these kinds of situations is to be tempered in our reactions. We feel the need to scream obscenities, but are wiser and more disciplined than that. We must remember that emotional rage only makes matters worse and remember that tragedies are rarely as bad as they seem, and even when they are, they give us an opportunity to grow stronger.

Create Your Mission Statement

Mine was simply "To translate what gives me joy, fulfillment and makes me genuinely happy into a career that will allow me to work for myself and spend more time with my family." This meant starting my own business as a coach to help individuals and small business owners get what they want out of their life and business. Formulating this sentence allows us to create a short mission statement that summarizes exactly what we want from life, which will help to keep it in the forefront of our minds when we're making important decisions.

Manage Your Time Better

Do you find yourself clicking on Facebook every ten minutes? Set a goal for yourself that you will refrain from going on any social media for an entire hour, then two hours. Your mind has a lot of control over your body. The more you tell yourself you're going to focus on your work, the more you actually will focus on your work.

"Until you make the unconscious conscious, it will direct your life and you will call it fate." — Carl Gustav Jung

Chapter 4. FOCUS

Your focus in anything is key, in order to get things done. It's that simple! I can relate to this subject more than most and I say this because I have been terrible at focusing, you would see me 'trying' to focus on one thing and then get distracted by my phone, the TV or other people's drama! Sound familiar? You cannot control what goes on around you however, you can control what you get affected by, yes it's down to you. Below I will give you some tips on how to really keep focused.

COMMITMENT

Achieving even the simplest of goals requires us to learn the meaning of commitment. Throughout our life, we are reminded of commitment, whether it's related to personal or business goals, and we realize that without committing, we can't achieve anything.

When you think about it, everything you ever achieved sprouted from a commitment you made; whether it's your children, your degree, your job, or even your house. Learning how to commit is not simply about making commitments, it's about keeping those commitments in the face of foreseen and unforeseen hurdles.

Commitment to Goals

There are many ways to stay committed to your goals so that you don't get side tracked. Often we write our goals down and then we just sit on them for a really long time or we keep focused for a while but then we end up hitting a brick wall, there could be a number of reasons why and one reason is your 'WHY' — it's the centre of everything you want to achieve. Are your goals big enough to scare you? Do you have an emotional connection to them (maybe think about the key people in your life) an example of my 'WHY' is to support my family or to have a better quality of life, if the answer is yes, keep reading below for tips on how to stay committed to them. If the answer is no, then a have a think about them and re-write them out then before you continue to read.

Make Them Practical

It's great to dream big; we need monumental, life-long goals for our lives to feel meaningful. But sometimes, when we're stuck in the daily routine, it's easy to lose sight of those goals. This is often when we give up, simply settling for mediocrity instead. So, instead of focusing on what you'd like to achieve in the next ten years, set an ambition, an achievable one, a goal for the next ten days.

My belief is that we tend to work harder when the end of a project is in sight. Therefore, it's extremely useful to break your goal up into smaller projects — challenging tasks you can achieve in the near-term with a little hard work. These "small wins" will help you stay motivated over the long run.

Plan It Out

When committing to a goal, we often feel empowered and excited; "Yeah! I'm going to be a millionaire! I set a goal!" If only it were that easy. We're very prone to getting discouraged and giving up when things don't go our way. Maybe you get a parking ticket that interferes with your goal of saving £500 one month.

And then you give up on saving because it all seems so futile; anticipate there's always an unplanned expense.

Setbacks are inevitable. No matter what your goal, something is going to interfere with you achieving it. The people who are most successful in life anticipate these setbacks and plan around them. They imagine working towards a goal and then predict all the obstacles that will get in their way; then they develop a plan for overcoming them. When you do this, you're much less likely to get discouraged. You just see obstacles as a part of the process.

Make It Public

When you publicly commit to a goal, you're in effect asking others to hold you accountable. We're often held accountable in our careers and in school, but when we set more personal goals, there's no one we have to answer to but ourselves. This makes it easy to save face and give up; no one has to know about our failure.

But when you tell those you care about what you're going to do, they're going to make sure you'll actually do it. Tell a friend or family member, "I'm going to save £300 this month, and I'd like you to put a note in your calendar to follow up with me in thirty days." Better yet, do this with several people. We hate disappointing other people, so suddenly the goal will become that much more important.

"Commitment is the glue that bonds you to your goals." — Jill Koeng

MAKING DECISIONS

To be able to make decisions in life you need to not over analyse as it only prolongs the decision making process. Do you have a hard time making decisions? What techniques do you use to help you make one?

I say this as I have a history of not being able to make decisions quickly. Sometimes decisions can be tough to make and therefore require more time. I can openly tell you that up until recently I went against my gut feeling and it cost me, so always ensure you follow at least some of the steps below:

Listen to Your Intuition

First and foremost, what is your gut telling you? Too many of us ignore that message, or warning, and then question why we didn't just go with our gut instinct in the first place, when things don't work out. That feeling is undeniable. Listen to it, act on it! It can sometimes be very easy to ignore your feelings and push them away however, ultimately this is about your happiness and if something doesn't feel right then maybe it's time for a change. Be honest with yourself and acknowledge those unsettled feelings; they are there to guide and support you.

Write in a Diary or Journal

I have found writing in a journal to be an incredible method for tuning into my intuition. Acting as a safe space to release emotions, work through problems, and process my thoughts, it can allow for greater self-discovery and understanding.

Next time you are having difficulty making a decision, pick up a pen and some paper and let the words flow out of you. Reflect on the situation, explore those feelings, and consider the bigger picture. This free-flowing use of personal writing can be a wonderful catalyst for removing blocks and letting your intuitive voice lead the way. Just let the words pour out.

Look back on Your Past Decisions

Did you learn or take away anything from your past decisions? Was there a lesson to be learnt? If you take a moment to look back on other decisions, chances are you will see how you came out ok after all and you stressed out for nothing.

Be prepared to roll with the changes: If you can remind yourself that just because you made this decision it doesn't necessarily mean things will turn out as planned. Go ahead and make it anyway, just be prepared for a plan B. This takes a little pressure off of you as well.

Weigh out the Pros and Cons if It's a Big Life Changing Decision

Weigh up all of them and don't leave any out. Is this decision going to hurt or affect anyone negatively? Is it a good idea for you to be doing whatever it is you are thinking about doing? List everything and have a look. One side should definitely outweigh the other.

Listen to Yourself Talk

Don't beat yourself up and repeatedly tell yourself you don't know what you're doing. Instead tell yourself that no matter what the outcome, you did the best you could with what you had. Tell yourself that you did the best at making this decision and no matter what, you are proud of yourself for doing so.

Just Do It

Whatever it is, once you have done the pros and cons and thought about it and beat it to death, just do it. If you have to take a big deep breath before you do, then do that and then leap. Say a little prayer if you have to but go ahead and make your decision and let it go!

"It is in your moments of decision that your destiny is shaped." — Tony Robbins

TAKING ACTION

It's all very good talking about having the right mindset and thinking positively, but without doing anything, nothing will be achieved and it really is as simple as that! It pains me to say that I have spent years of procrastinating and thinking about how I wanted my life to be, without actually doing anything about it. If I had only got some support/guidance and stepped up and taken action! However it is never too late to work on your dreams. People often (and I was guilty of this too) say things like 'I'm too young' or 'I'm too old' 'I don't have the skills or confidence' — sound familiar?

If you think about it logically, when we're born, did we know how to talk or walk? No, everything we learnt was through practising and falling over again and again, and through determination and focus we got there in the end. The same applies with achieving your dreams, the only difference is that we have this voice in our heads that tells us we can't which has come from the influences of the media, society and our very own thoughts! So how can you overcome this need to procrastinate over things, which prevents you from moving forward? Here's how:

Take Daily Actions

Dreaming is nothing without action. Take daily actions to turn your big dream into reality. No matter how small, every action you take gets you one step closer to your big dream, and every day you take action you build momentum. A small action every day might not feel significant at the time, but over time little things add up. Just imagine what you could achieve in a year if you did one small thing every single day to move toward your big dream!

Put a Time Frame to It

Time flies, and if you haven't set a time frame on something, the hours, days, weeks and months, can easily escape you. Put a time frame on your big dream to keep yourself moving and accountable. The best way to do this is to set a launch date and then work backwards, setting specific dates to reach milestones along the way.

Ignore the Naysayers

Whenever you pursue a big dream there will always be naysayers who will tell you it can't be done. They might be your friends and family, but just because you hold them dear to your heart doesn't mean they are right. Often when people say something can't be done it's only because in their personal experience it hasn't been possible. Don't listen to them; you are a unique individual with the drive, motivation and ability to achieve your big dream.

Share Your Dream with Others

Don't keep your big dream locked away, share it with others. While not everyone will get on board with it, there will be those who do, and these people can be a huge help to you in achieving your dream. The people who believe in you will boost you up when you are down, keep you motivated and inspired, and put you in touch with the right people when you need it most.

Make Room for Your Big Dream

For your big dream to flourish, you need to make room for it in your life. You need to clear out everything that no longer serves you and make the time and space to work on your big dream. This might mean clearing other commitments from your diary or creating a home office space, or even clearing your phone book, make room for more like-minded people in your life that will support and encourage you with your vision.

Keep the Momentum Going

The most important step to achieving a big dream is keeping the momentum going. Every day that you take action toward achieving your big dream, you build your momentum and get one step closer. Once you've got momentum on your side you become an unstoppable force and success becomes imminent.

"Awareness without action is worthless." — Phil McGraw

COMFORT ZONE

Ah that good old comfort zone, one thing I can tell you now, is that if you stay stuck in it, you're limiting yourself. You are less likely to reach your full potential, I know that's not what you want to hear but it's true.

I've realized that after spending time outside my comfort zone, it feels so much better when you do go back to life inside your comfort zone. It feels as though you have really earnt it and the small things you took for granted previously, such as spending a night at home relaxing and watching movies provide you with much more pleasure.

I wouldn't say I'm an expert of jumping out of that comfort zone but I do have some right to talk about it. One of the biggest achievements of this year relating to stepping out of my comfort zone was when I did a skydive to raise money for charity. I didn't think even in my wildest dreams I would actually do this, but one day I decided I would, I booked it and just went for it.

I won't go into explaining the details of the experience (for those who would like to try it I don't want to spoil it for you), but I will tell you one thing, mentally my mind has developed so much, because I stretched myself to do something I didn't anticipate doing. I'm not suggesting that you all must jump off a plane, but what I am saying is that you should do even the smallest things you can do to push yourself.

Here are many ways to get out of that comfort zone. I'm not saying you should stick to these methods, but they give you an idea. Stepping out of the comfort zone needn't mean taking massive actions, the small things can still really stretch you.

Move through Fear with Action

Use your fears to challenge yourself to new heights. The best antidote to fear is taking action. Take an adventurous approach to anything you fear. Are you afraid to fly on airplanes and as a result, keep missing out on family holidays? Are you afraid to invest time, energy and money into a business idea you've had for a long time? Get some objective advice about best business practices for your idea and then step out in faith. Are you afraid to speak in front of groups? Perhaps you could join Toast Masters and learn how to speak in a group where everyone else is also learning.

Visualise Yourself Reaching that Next Level of Success

The brain can more easily create new neural pathways when we engage as many of the senses as possible, so create a mental movie that is rich in detail. What would it look like when you reach that major goal? What kinds of sights, smells, tastes and feelings will you experience once you reach that goal? Take a few five minute breaks throughout the day to relax with deep breaths and run your mental movie. The more you visualise yourself accomplishing your goal, the more likely you are to move out of your comfort zone to create the new thoughts and behaviours needed to succeed.

Invest Money into Your Personal Development

When times are tight, our knee-jerk reaction is to tend to cut back on classes, coaching, or counselling. Instead of giving in to the temptation to slash growth-producing spending, find some savvy ways to invest in your personal development. This will signal your own psyche that you value yourself as a wonderfully created being and that you have faith in yourself to grow to new heights in life, love and work.

If you need help moving out of your comfort zone, consider investing in counselling, business or career coaching, mentoring, or consult an objective person who will help you set new goals and reach for the stars. Make this phrase your life mantra, "Feel the fear, and do it anyway!"

Focus on the 'How' not 'If''

What ifs can really mess with your mind. You can spend days, weeks or years thinking about what may happen if you take action. So instead of letting your mind get lost in what ifs, focus on the how. In a situation, focus on how you can do something how you can solve a problem or achieve a goal. Do some research if you need to, or get support and help from others.

Focusing on the how puts your mind to better use and creates a positive attitude within rather than a negative and uncertain one. This makes it easier to take action without too much hand wringing and time spent over-thinking things.

'Choose' Instead of 'Should'

Here's a small but useful tip. You don't really need to do anything. You always choose what to do. Thinking about things this way removes the 'shoulds' and 'need to dos' that take your personal power away and make you feel like you aren't in control. When you think that you choose to do whatever you do then you regain the control and power. And it becomes easier to take action. This is something I learnt the hard way and found myself doing things because I thought it would make me successful or make me more money — I was wrong.

"You can only grow if you are willing to feel awkward and uncomfortable when you try something NEW." — Brain Tracey

Chapter 5. ENVIRONMENT

You may not realise but your environment influences your success, you are affected by the people you spend most of your time with. Now have a think about the people in your life, are these people positive, driven and supportive? If the answer is yes then great, but if it's no, then why are they still in your life? I also want to talk about the importance of a balanced environment and what I mean by that is the work-life balance, it's easy to talk about but I do understand at times, it can be difficult to put in place. If you don't have this balance, in the long term you will suffer! I strongly believe that in order to be productive in achieving your life's ambitions you need that balance, it's as simple as that.

HOUSEHOLD

You could argue maybe that family members, I can relate to this, don't share your vision or your beliefs. That's ok, they don't have to; they just need to understand or respect them as you do theirs, right? Sometimes they make demands on you or your time, how this is managed is through clear communication and ensuring that there is a healthy balance between work and family, here are some pointers to help you deal with family:

Let Your Family Members Be as They Are

Give them space. I mean this even if you are sitting with them — give them space to simply be. Don't take any responsibility for what they say or do, and do not take any responsibility for your own reactions. I often do exactly the same, the moment you start to take it in and let it attract you, that's when you're in trouble!

When These Waves of Unpleasant Feelings Arise in You

Let these be as well, do not identify with them. Be the neutral space of awareness in which feelings arise. Be a witness to them, let them be. Treating feelings in this way will begin to remove their power over you. Negativity cannot survive in an accepting, surrendered, alert inner state.

You Cannot Control Someone Else's Negativity or Opinions

If you argue against it, you just make it worse. However you can use it to burn up any latent negativity inside yourself. With family members in particular, negativity can be triggered inside you, or trigger shared negativity that exists within many members of the group — which you can then transcend using awareness and non-resistance (surrender/acceptance).

Take Time for Yourself

If you are forced to live with negative or problem-orientated family members, then make sure you get enough alone time to relax, rest, and recuperate. Having to play the role of a 'focused, rational adult' in the face of toxic moodiness can be exhausting, and if you're not careful, the toxicity can infect you. Again, understand that even people with legitimate problems can still comprehend that you have needs as well, which means you can politely excuse yourself when you need to.

WORKPLACE

Now, negativity in the workplace. That's something that I know quite a lot about. I've had much experience of it over the last ten years. There have been all sorts of negativity; from bosses, to colleagues, and just the negative environment around. Of course, the environment is what we're talking about at the moment. There are many reasons why people are negative, it could be that they are going through a negativity phase or something is taking place in their life.

In these situations you just need to be more mindful and not let it rub off on you, because more often than not, it's not personal. That's something that I used to have an issue with for a very long time, which is not to take things personally. When I used to go into work, I would find that when I had looked at someone who didn't look happy, every word that came out of their mouth was negative, and I'd think to myself, do I take this personally? They're a bit snappy, or they looked at me in a funny way, or they didn't say hello to me this morning. How do I take this? Is it to do with me? The answers is no!

It's easily manageable and not as difficult as we think. The first thing I'd say is, turn barriers into opportunities. Look at negative behaviours and attitudes as opportunities for improvement. Now, instead of dreading these issues, you can maintain your own positive attitude by controlling your response. Obviously, you can't control the other person, so start with yourself. Often negativity starts with negative self-talk.

Turn Negativity into Positivity

Replace any negative self-talk with positive self-talk. You could do this for yourself, or you can suggest it to someone else, if you think that you're friendly with the person. You've known them quite well. Negative thoughts, obviously lead to self-doubt and failure, as we have already established. Look for negative thinking in, not just yourself, but other people, because you can always look at someone else's negativity in a positive light in your own head, if that makes sense. For example say to yourself, they might be going through a tough time. It's not great for them at the moment, but I'm not going to let that affect me.

Talk It through

If you know that the person is going through things, lend them an ear, talk to them about it. See if you can actually help them, or seek help for them. Taking action to build trust will increase comfort levels and strengthen relationships. So build that trust with that person. I can tell you, from my own past that I've had experiences where someone's being negative, and I've tried to be positive. They ended up confiding in me, and I've found out many things about them that I never knew, had I not spoken to them and built that rapport.

Win People to Your Way of Thinking

Now that's something I've already touched upon, where a person looks at you and thinks, "they're always happy and always smiling." The only way to win an argument is to avoid it, when handled correctly, that is. Disagreements and debates are opportunities for positive change. When disagreements arise, show respect for the other person's opinion. Obviously avoid shouting, or biting back, instead try to oppose, or put in a strong debate against what they're saying. It's always about respecting other people's opinions. They may have strong opinions about something in the workplace or in life in general. You just have to appreciate and respect their opinions.

Disagree Agreeably

The key question is how do we disagree agreeably and still have our ideas heard as well? When you're in meetings, for example, keep the lines of communication open, by trying to see things through a different perspective, as I've mentioned. Really take time to think about how the other person thinks, and what they feel and why they feel the way they do, because again, it could be as a result of many things. Just the way they see things, or particular reasons, their background, whatever the case may be, you just never know.

Don't Say the Person Is Wrong

I would suggest not under any circumstances to say to someone they are wrong! Try to see things through their point of view. In the past I'd always been in this position where I've not seen things from the other person's point of view, and I jumped to my own conclusions, built up stories in my head. This is making assumptions without knowing the story or the facts. You've got to try and see it through the other person's point of view. At the end of the day, you don't have to accept their opinions and it's not a competition to see who is right, you just have to appreciate or respect them. That can avoid rubbing off negativity from an environment or the workplace.

I hope that gives you enough to help you with in the workplace. If you are experiencing severe problems, which may be considered as bullying or you think you're being indirectly bullied, this is something to take up with a line manager at work.

Social Media

There can be times when you may face negative people on social media. If you get into a position whereby you are being attacked or criticised then it is important to follow this advice.

Social media is a unique public environment. It's got its own culture, and expectations. It's different from traditional customer service, and public relations, which isn't enough so we use social media to promote our business, build relationships, networking, etcetera. It's a brilliant tool, social media is, to do those things. Sometimes you can achieve far more from building your network through social media, which is obviously through different sites such as Facebook, Twitter, LinkedIn, obviously there's many to name but I won't go into that now... I wouldn't say I've experienced much negativity via social media, but I've seen how my other friends on Facebook have. How some people that I'm friends with have actually shown their negativity towards other people and the way they work.

Evidence

Have some evidence so that you can support yourself, and stand up for yourself. Criticizers are out there, negative people, haters or whatever you want to call them. I think it's good to have feedback and use it in a positive way, for example, if an individual has criticized your website, or made comments about it, do not take it personally and do not let it get to you. Instead use that information to improve things. We all love it and it makes us feel good when people say nice or positive things about us, don't we.

Being a coach myself, if someone was to post something negative I would probably say, I appreciate your comments, or thank you for your feedback, I respect your opinion, or something along those lines. Then take the conversation offline and speak to the person, to try and find out the true reasons for their negativity.

Keep Your Cool

It's not uncommon that an offended customer, client, or internet user is trying to get an emotional reaction or response from their post. It is critical that you do not take this personally when engaging, or challenging that person. Remember this is in public, and you are being judged by not only your post, but all your followers. Act as if you were responding to an angry mob, but being right might not be the end goal. That's not always the end goal.

Tone

A pleasant, positive, playful tone creates an atmosphere where aggressive or negativity attacks will seem out of place. In this scenario it's even possible that your other followers will come to your defence so that you don't have to. On the other hand, avoid sounding like an authority, and don't be a smart Alec, as the internet is always smarter. Always, always be careful with the tone of your post in response as well. Consider another avenue for complaints, chances are the client is not seeking to rat you out on social media sites.

Choose Your Battles Carefully

You don't have to reply to everything. If the comment is clearly an attack on an effort to pick a fight, let it go. Simple as — just let it go. Believe me, I'm talking from experience here. Luckily I've not had a lot of negative comments, but certain friends of mine, and people that I work with have. Associates, coaches, business people, it happens. It will happen in the future, it is inevitable. Another thing I'd like to say is check your head. Social media is just like any other social experience to the extent that it's not always clever to answer. It is chaotic, and unpredictable, just like any other social experience that you might have face to face or over the phone to someone offline.

It's nice to be able to speak to someone sometimes to see where they're coming from and equally important for them to find out where you're coming from. I hope these tips have helped you to handle social media. I guarantee you, whether you are a business owner, or in another field of work, you will be using social media as one of your marketing tools. It is therefore highly important to put yourself across in the right way.

Use these tips to help you in getting forward from dealing with negativity on social media.

WORK-LIFE BALANCE

Life balance and personal happiness do not necessarily depend on earning more money and being successful at work or in business. Other things can have a much bigger impact on our well-being.

Our life balance is constantly changing and different. There is no single model that's right for everyone, and no single approach is right for anyone for their whole life. The search for happiness is further complicated because the factors which most affect our personal well-being are commonly ignored or given very low priority in work and training, and in the media too. In schools also, life balance and personal happiness are largely ignored, and rarely explored or recommended as worth pursuing.

Consequently throughout our lives we don't find it easy to properly consider the issues which actually determine our own personal life balance and happiness. Like most other things however, life balance and happiness can be managed and attained, if we know the components — including our true self — and the causes of our own well-being.

Life balance can therefore be understood, planned and achieved, just like any other important aim. The ideas in this book attempt to illustrate the wide range of factors affecting our life balance and personal happiness — and whatever these concepts mean to you. And there is also a simple tool to assist the process of considering and making some changes towards a happier more balanced life.

For many people life balance equates simply to personal happiness. For others life balance is far more complex. Life balance also depends on your situation — and your age or life stage. Life balance is expressed in many different ways, for example:

- Work-Life balance
- Fulfilment — and personal or emotional fulfilment
- Well-being and personal well-being/wellbeing
- Happiness or simply being happy
- At peace (with myself or life) or in harmony with life
- Contentment and inner calm

Time Management

Time management is a crucial aspect of life balance and personal well-being. A powerful illustration of our ability to manage time better, so as to enjoy a better balance, is the ruthless approach we tend to apply to time management on the days before our annual leave. Imagine how much more balanced your life could be if you always managed your time as efficiently.

Manage Your Environment

The ways we use mobile phones and emails significantly influence our living and working environment — and specifically external pressures and demands on us.

"These otherwise positive communication technologies have become for many people habits and systems which enslave and constrain, rather than liberate and enable." — Kam Bedi

Left unmanaged and uncontrolled, mobile phones, emails, and increasingly laptops and blackberry-type gadgets, make us constantly available, constantly attentive and forever distracted. This is fine if it makes you happy, but what if it doesn´t?

Manage your environment — don't let your environment — external factors like mobile phones and emails — manage you. Make the change — ensuring you explain your new ways of working to those who need to know. A simple change to make with emails is to open them and deal with them, at set times during the day, not whenever one pops into your inbox or on your notification bar. A simple change to make for a mobile phone is to get rid of it. Or hit it with a great big bloody hammer. That'll sort it! Failing that try switching it off when you want some time for yourself, or merely turn it to flight mode or ′do not disturb′ for an hour or so.

Communications technologies are meant to make your life easier, not more stressed and difficult. Control these things. Manage your environment. Don't allow external factors — especially your habits and expectations and assumptions of others — to manage you.

Manage Other People's Expectations

We all get into habits which form the expectations and views that other people hold about us. Other people's demands on our emotional and time resources are a significant aspect of life balance. If you do not manage these demands they will leave you with no resources for yourself, your loved ones, your other passions in life, and the changes you want to make in order to pursue them.

"One of the best ways to make changes in your life is to change your environment. This then changes you." — Robert Kiyosaki

Chapter 6. INSPIRATION

What does inspiration really mean? What does inspiration mean to you? In the context of personal development, I can explain this.

I'd say inspiration comes from everywhere. You can get inspired by your surroundings and people such as your parents, your friends, your siblings and teachers. Everyone has their own qualities, their own motivation and their own personalities. Like I was saying in the previous chapter, everyone's an individual. Everyone's got unique talents and gifts.

For example, when you see the success of a team at work or someone overcoming an obstacle in their path, it is because they push through. As I mentioned our parents can be our great inspiration, how they have dedicated their whole lives to make us successful, to make sure that we've got everything and encourage us to become the person that we really want to be.

Inspiration is a word brought about by other human beings. They show by their activities how inspirational they are. You can be the inspiration for this, where they will be motivated by your personality. It works both ways. You could be inspired by other people in the way they work, in the way they do things, the way they live their life, having said that, we also could be the inspiration for other people. It works both ways.

The knowledge inside you gives you the inspiration. It comes from everywhere. I'm going to discuss it in this chapter, which will cover concepts such as role models, those in your life that you can say, "I'm so inspired by this person and what they've done and what they've achieved." "I'd like to be like them." Maybe they're around. Maybe they're not around, but either way, it doesn't mean that they're haven't left a mark in this world to offer inspiration.

BOOKS

There are so many books out there. I've read loads and I know some people that I work with, coaches and business owners, that have read over 300 books. The thing about reading books is you don't just read the book and then put it to one side. They are there for you to take something from them, learn from them, put strategies into practice in your own life and follow through. There could be things in them that make you think "wow that resonates with me. That's something I'm going to include in my daily life as I go on."

With books, you read them to personally develop yourself, to get inspiration or most importantly, to become the inspiration. With reading books, as I mentioned, you don't just read them, you put practices into actions.

Joy of Learning

I have a profound curiosity about people, the meaning of life and our purpose here on Earth, and what different people have to say about it. Learning about these things makes me happy.

Humility

The more I read, study, and learn, the more I realise that I do not have all of the answers. In fact, *"pulling one thread of questioning often leads to the unraveling of your entire life philosophy"*, — Kam Bedi

This in turn leads to more study and reflection. I have learned that I am not the final word on anything.

Self-Acceptance

This is one of the most liberating results of my self-help pursuits. Through all of my reading and study, especially of people like Byron Katie and Eckhart Tolle, I've come to like and accept myself just as I am.

Conflict Resolution

Learning to handle conflict, especially in your love relationship, is a skill that must be mastered. It doesn't come naturally to most of us. Left to our own devices, we are like children fighting over candy.

Prioritizing

Personal development reading has helped me prioritize what is *most* important in my life. You can't do or have everything, and this knowledge has forced me to sit down and make tough decisions about where I want to focus my time and energy. I am so much more productive now in areas I really like.

WORKSHOPS/SEMINARS

The word itself, 'workshop', to me means you put the work in. You go into a workshop for example, to build confidence. Around that, you would conduct activities based around building your confidence, activities interacting with other people. Again, you learn something and you take something away. You don't just forget about it and say "I went to this workshop, and it was really great," and then you don't implement anything. Implementation is absolutely key, in carrying forward your inspiration and your growth.

Seminars are slightly different. There is some interaction but seminars provide you with information about something you may be interested in. For example, it's very common nowadays for people to hold meditation or motivational practices. Anything that you're into, you can attend seminars to really better develop yourself.

You may have heard of the term *junkies* when it comes to personal development. However, this simply refers to people who attend course after course, much like me, who used to be that person. But did you ever stop and think about why these people are so enthusiastic about attending these workshops and seminars? I'll continue now talking about the benefits of workshops and seminars going forward.

Broaden Your Knowledge

First, self-development workshops can broaden a person's scope. I have attended many and every time I learn to see things from different angles and perspectives. It actually makes you think deeper, rather than accepting things at their face value. It teaches you to ask questions like, "Who? When? Where? What? Why? How?"

Make You Think More

I would even say that they develop your cognitive thinking because they make you want to think more. You may even notice how other people fail to see things from your perspective and that is where you need to realize that these people do not have the privilege of learning the stuff that you learn at the seminar.

Develop Existing Skills

The next benefit of attending personal development courses is pretty obvious, and that is the fact that you get to improve yourself. I have mentioned this point previously in the paragraph above, but apart from broadening your scope, workshops can also help you develop your interpersonal skills and emotional quotient. There are even some events where you will be forced to step out of your comfort zone and do things that you either fear or dread doing. Hence, you may even overcome your fears at such events.

Opportunity to Meet New People

Personal development courses also give you the opportunity to meet like-minded people. This is your chance to network with people who have the same interests as you and form lifelong friendships. You could even take this a step further by becoming business partners or starting a joint venture together. The possibilities are endless. Most of the speakers in these workshops will encourage you to mix with other people. However, I encourage you to take the initiative to socialize and get to know others. Once you have made friends during the event, I encourage you to keep in touch with them after the event is over. It would be a waste to meet someone at an event and fail to keep in touch with them later.

YOU OWN INSPIRATION

Inspiration can come from many things; it can come from just sitting down and meditating for a few minutes. It can come from being in nature, which is something I have become quite a big fan of. I'll go outside for a break and I'll sit there and breathe. Something will just come to you.

Sometimes, you don't have to be around people, reading, listening to audios, or attending seminars. You may be in your own little space, in your own little world, (I'd recommend spending at least five to ten minutes a day, every day to yourself, if not more, if you're able to). I understand that people have busy schedules and it can be difficult, but it makes a real difference just being there with you and your thoughts in a peaceful environment.

Self-inspiration is the ability to take yourself from bored to passionate, from stagnant to active, from discouraged to excited. It doesn't depend on external assistance. Self-inspiring people can inspire themselves (and likely others) anytime and anywhere. Self-inspiring people get things done.

Inspiration doesn't always need to come from within, but most of it should. To depend on external stimuli to inspire you will frequently leave you disappointed and unproductive. You won't always find the perfect article. Your friends won't always know the magical words to say to you.

ROLE MODEL

Finding a role model is the next step. A positive role model is someone who has the most powerful tools. We have to find happiness and success in life. We often find these treasures as we go through childhood. We find them in our family, schools and churches. We cling to their example, their spirit, and their knowledge. However, as we move through different phases in our lives, we have different needs. We need guidance in our career, raising our own children, and simply finding our changing place in the world. Positive role models are not just for young children and troubled teens. Even as adults, we benefit greatly from experience of those with character and purpose, and that's important.

To continue, I'll give you some tips on how to find a role model. A role model can be easy to find once you know the kind of influence and guidance you need in your life. Everybody's different, so I would say a wonderful statement about the world around us is that there are role models everywhere. It could be to do with your personal life it could be to do with your career, your health, and fitness. You can find a role model, as a general rule, in all areas of life.

Good people with sincerely good intentions abound every day. You pass them by in the street, at the grocery store, or while driving through your neighbourhood. Unfortunately, these can be difficult to discover and connect with. However, these are places that allow for better opportunities to find a role model to help you strengthen your resolve, your confidence, your hope, and your life.

Where are they? Where can you find these role models? You can find them on the job. The workplace can be a source of stress caused by endless demands and hectic schedules. It can also be a place where role models are found, yes, it can happen. There may be quite a few of you that don't see any role models in the workplace, but I think in terms of what I was saying about 'on the job', the typical work week often results in more time spent with co-workers than with your own families, if you think about it, particularly if you're doing a nine 'til five job where you spend most of your week at work. That's five days a week, forty hours a week, on average. You may as well try and make the most of it, right? There are usually a few that stand out as conscientious and hard-working. They're goal orientated, and you can always spot these people. These have the potential for being great role models both professionally and personally.

At the Workplace

Seeking advice and direction from someone you admire at work is a good choice if you are searching for guidance on career goals and decisions. These types of role models will be more knowledgeable and honest than friends and family about how your choices may affect your job, and further career. In a sense, friends and family can be helpful, but they don't always make the best role models because they are so familiar with you. The workplace is not the only source that may surround us with role models on a daily basis. Other places where you find yourself often, such as your child's school, football practice, just off the top of my head, and the gym, are all filled with others living similar lives and going through similar struggles.

A Parent/Friend

Another example of a role model, a parent is a wonderful place to turn for advice and support with all that is involved with raising children in today's world. The elderly or very overweight person at the gym, for example, that never gives up, and continues to work hard for their health is admirable and can be very motivating when you feel yourself abandoning your goal. Look around you. You may realize that your next door neighbour, good friend or favourite aunt have the characteristics you want to emulate. You may be laughing at the part about the aunt, I know I was. All of these ordinary people have found a successful way to navigate the worries and trials of life. Connect with them. Learn their secrets, and let them help motivate you to find similar success and peace.

Specialist in Your Field

The really important advice about finding a role model is looking to someone who's specialized in their field. If you are looking for a role model because of a particular battle that you are fighting such as addiction, illness or depression, you know local groups are an excellent place to start. There are several groups and organizations that are focused on helping others overcome life's struggles and supply a constant support.

Each of these relate to survivors that offer experience and care to those that are really trying to recover. Quite often these groups are centred in your company; they could be in your church or local neighbourhood. This further magnifies the realization you are not alone. When this unity is combined with admirable leaders the potential for success is high.

Another one I'd like to mention is in a business capacity. If you're looking for someone to model yourself on and if you're a budding entrepreneur, business owner, change maker, whatever you want to call yourself, the best way to go is to get yourself either a coach or find yourself a mentor who's obviously been through that whole journey of becoming the person you want to become and actually help you through every step of the way.

For example, someone who's a specialist in business coaching and you want to become a business coach, it would be wise to find someone who's already made it there so you can just basically follow their steps for success. However ensure to bring your own personality in, have your own twist to things, that's really important. Always use the strategies and make them your own.

Yourself

The most important 'role model' I'd like to talk about the person you see in the mirror — you! Now life has a tendency to make us focus on our failures and weaknesses. However, we all have success and strength in our lives. It is possible to discover these by really examining yourself. You may already be a positive role model for someone else and you might not have even realized it up until now, when I've mentioned it.

For example the father that is fighting for a promotion may not feel successful but to his child he may be a shining example of diligence and hard work. Have you been in a position where you know, that when you were younger if you can remember, your dad put in all the hours and worked so hard to give you the best life he could and he probably felt not only exhausted and stressed but still felt like he wasn't doing his best whereas in your eyes he was. So you never know where you can find that source of a role model.

Understanding the positive impact you have on another person's life can be just as empowering as the advice and guidance of your own role model. The greatest aspect of a positive role model is the fullness in which it can affect your life. A role model that is supporting and guiding you in career decisions will probably have many other positive traits to share with you too. The manager you admire at work may also be an active parent and devoted to his job.

A positive role model is the gift that keeps on giving. The example of good character can lead to an endless number of ethical decisions and conscientious actions of others. Role models benefit everyone and are not difficult to find. Our everyday lives are filled with people who live with purpose, confidence and perseverance and those are the people that you really want to be following. Tapping into their perspective and experience will guide you through many of life's challenges.

This allows you to understand the reasoning behind how your role model treats others and makes decisions, which is really important, so definitely take in what I've just said.

Knowing where their character's coming from keeps you from merely copying your role model. That allows you to truly transform your way of thinking and living in the way that you want, so that's the way to do it. Keep your eyes open and you will discover the guidance you may need could be right in front of you.

AUDIOS

Audio books are similar to reading books, but in a sense they are slightly different. Normally I prefer to read a book, and it may seem like a strange concept at first listening to someone read a book, but for me my first introduction to an audio book was when I was reading a Tony Robbins book and let me tell you I was captivated! It felt as if someone was reading me a bedtime story. It's magical and I haven't stopped since!

I also try and listen to an audio ranging anything from five to twenty minutes each day but it all depends on the person and their lifestyle, whether you can walk around freely, in the park, around your house, just walk around anywhere you want listening to it.

Better Engagement

I would like to go through a few benefits of audio books and similarly books. There are self-help audios out there, some of which I've put links to at the bottom of this section. One of the things I'd say is that audio books can help you engage better. I have heard many people say that their mind wanders when they're listening to a book. They can't focus and they lose the story. This happens to me on occasions, but honestly it happens no matter how I read. Just like I can swipe or turn a page to go back if I started planning dinner mid story, I can easily tap the back button and go back a few seconds at a time and just go from there, so it's not a problem.

Multi Task

Another benefit of audio books is you can listen to them while you do other things, like I mentioned. One of the reasons I feel I don't do as much reading as I want is because it's so exclusive. You have to have your full attention on the book. With an audio book, obviously, not every task lends itself to thoughtful listening, but there are plenty of things that can be done while listening to an audio book. I like to listen when I'm doing things like graphic designs, you know, any little projects. It could be drawing. It could be all sorts of things.

Chores Become More Fun

Another benefit of audio books is that it makes a boring task more interesting. This kind of goes with the previous one, but think about all those menial tasks you do during the day such as the dishes, folding laundry, cleaning. These things can all be boring, but if you listen to an audio book while you do them, you'll forget that you're supposed to be bored. Dishes are much more interesting when I do them while listening to an audio by one of my favourite inspirational coaches or speakers.

Faster Pace

Another benefit is that you can read faster. Maybe this isn't a factor for you if you're a fast reader, I know, however, I'm not, and I feel like it takes me forever just to get from one page to another, no matter how interesting a book may be. With audios the pace is faster and there's less time required to internalize the words, at least for me.

Below I have included a few links of audio books which I think you will find really, really interesting in terms of personal development and inspiration on the go:

- *Rewire Your Brain* — John B. Arden
- *Mind Body Mastery* — Dan Millman
- *The 7 Habits of Highly Effective People* — Steven Convey

MEDITATION

We live in a crazy, connected age. Our minds are constantly being bombarded with information — via the internet, TV, mobile phones, Blackberrys, instant messaging, Twittering, Facebook, advertising, newspapers, friends — and work. It's no wonder that we can begin to feel overwhelmed and overloaded at times.

Quieten the Mind

One of the key benefits of meditation is that it totally clears and quietens your mind. The constant mind chatter that runs through your head all day begins to slow and with practice will almost disappear.

Instead, you will be left with a peaceful and quiet internal space for deeper contemplation and relaxation. You will also begin to notice a dimension of space in your mind that obliterates your day-to-day stresses.

Even twenty minutes of visiting this quiet and peaceful place is enough to 'reset' your system and make you feel more relaxed, calm and focussed. Believe me — it's a wonderful place to visit.

If you're susceptible to mood swings, stress, anxiety or feelings of being overwhelmed — meditation will help calm you, clear your mind and feel more in control.

Understand Yourself Better

We all want to understand ourselves better and answer the key questions in life — Why are we here? What is my purpose? What sort of person am I? In fact, we can spend far too much time debating these questions consciously — with very little in the way of progress.

Meditation allows for deeper contemplation than regular thought. When you are in a relaxed, higher state of consciousness, it is a lot easier to take a more objective look at yourself and your life — and see things from a new perspective.

Meditation can also help you to distance yourself from some of the automatic responses that occur in your brain — which make you act in a certain unconscious way. With practice, you will learn how to control your brain consciously — something that the majority of people fail to do.

Good For: If you've ever wanted to understand yourself better, control your thinking patterns, take charge of your emotions and begin to realise why you act the way you do, meditation is a fantastic way to go about it.

Good for Your Health

There are numerous scientific studies into the health benefits of meditation. Mainstream science, of late, appears to be catching up with all the Zen folks who have been evangelising the positive health benefits of meditation for years.

From first-hand experience, I can honestly say that meditation has strengthened my immune system — I get ill less, have more energy — and I'm sure my memory is improving too.

All of these observations back up recent scientific studies. Whilst I'd encourage you to do your own experimentation, the following health benefits of meditation seem to be readily accepted — decreased stress and anger; increased happiness; greater resistance to colds and illness; increased relaxation.

"Inspiration is finding something that excites you." — Connie Smith

Chapter 7. SUPPORT/NETWORK

We know that there are many ways to build a support network, and what I mean by that is people that are going to be there for you through all of your experiences, good and bad, especially when you're trying to get on the journey of personal development. It can be difficult and you can feel alone sometimes so it's always good to have people around you. Supportive people could come in the form of your close family or your friends, I would recommend getting yourself a coach, find the best coach that you can that you can afford and work with them to help you set your goals, make a plan of action, and actually go ahead and do those things that you have been continually putting off.

The benefits of having a support network can ease your stress by providing many kinds of practical emotional support. The other one is more enjoyment of life.

Everybody needs both time alone, and time with others. A strong personal support network will help to ensure that you'll have companionship when you would prefer to share an activity with others. It's a sense of belonging; you're less likely to feel alone if you spend time with people who value, and care about you. Whether they are your favourite cousins, former class mates, members of the community, or work colleagues, they can be a number of different people.

Peace of Mind

You'll have a stronger sense of security if you have people in your life who you know would be willing to pick you up. A support network doesn't just help you, it lets you help others too and that is so important. I have to emphasize that, even if you are doing fine, you may gain some self-confidence from helping other people who are struggling with challenges that you've already overcome, and things that you've had to experience in the past, or are overcoming at this very point in time.

One of the biggest rewards is when you help someone else. I myself also help people, whether it's through having a telephone conversation, face to face meetings or catch ups.

Better Health

Many studies have found that strong ties to others can improve your health, and may even possibly help you live longer. Don't quote me on that, that's just something that I have just researched. You can always find out more information by doing some research yourself if you wish.

Mutual Appreciation and Desire to Help

Members give as much as they receive, so strengthening your network begins with willing to go out of your way to help others. Think about your current relationships, are you giving others the kind of support that you would like to have, or may need some day? If not, look for ways to start doing more for people who may need your help. This will also strengthen your current support network.

Keep in Touch

If you don't keep in touch with others you may not stay up to date on the kind of support that people in your network need. You may also find it harder to ask for support when you need it. You could email, or send someone a message, asking how they are, it's that simple. Consider joining online networks that your friends and family enjoy. Online networks can strengthen your support system as long as they don't replace other forms of communication.

Going online is a great way to stay connected. Some social media sites let you see new posts by your friends, even if you post rarely they can help you stay up to date on other activities. Social media is great, but don't forget the other ways of communicating: which are face to face, telephone, spending time with people that you really appreciate and have in your network. Be loyal, respect the confidence of people in your network and never spread information about them that may be hurtful or untrue.

This will help to show them that they can trust you, and talk easily about their needs. I've experienced similar incidents where I've heard things but have chosen nonetheless to keep them to myself. It's just to make sure that no one else gets hurt by you sharing information with other people when it's sensitive stuff to do with their lives.

Remember special days; call or send a card, birthday card, anniversary, holidays and other days that are important to people in your network. Keep in mind that even if you would prefer to ignore your own birthdays and some holidays, many people need extra support at these times. It's actually nice where again, you can send someone a birthday card for example by post, or you can just send it online. Also have a positive outlook; people are usually more willing to support someone who tries to stay cheerful, even if he or she may be having difficulties than someone who is always complaining.

Show Family and Friends that They Are Important to You

Return their calls and messages and respond to invitations promptly. Tell them frequently that you appreciate them. Even those who support you strongly may back off if they sense that you aren't interested in the relationship. It is always nice now and again, to appreciate people and let them know. Again, you can do that in different ways, but face to face is always the nicest and most effective way. That's another point that I come to which is to make time for face to face get togethers, even if you prefer to communicate by phone, text message, or email. Others may be more willing to open up in a face to face conversation. If you never or rarely see each other you may not fully understand how you can help, or have a chance to talk about your needs. If possible have an annual get together, that's just as an example. Obviously it depends on how you, your family and friends work together. I mean what the interactions are like, what your views are, but a barbecue or holiday are nice ways of allowing you to get more connected with family and relatives that you haven't seen in a while.

Thank People for Their Support

Say thank you often and remind people of things that they have done in the past that you appreciated. Make an extra effort to show your gratitude when people go out of their way to support you. Send a card, note, flowers, or give a small gift. It doesn't have to be big it could be the smallest gesture. One of the nicest things I've found to be honest is to actually just make a cake. I love baking, I find it so therapeutic, so that's another way you can show your appreciation, just bake something. Try it one day, just something small, something nice. Whether it's buying a thank you card, or baking a cake, whatever it is that you can think of that you're able to do. It's the smallest things that count it doesn't have to be a huge gesture. Show all those people that you appreciate their support.

In addition to strengthening your current network you may also want to bring new people into your network. I'll just go through that with you. Be open to relationships with a variety of people, avoid assuming that people in your network need to share all your interests and values, they don't. Sometimes you have to be more open to other people's views and values. Not saying that you have to become best friends, or become really, really close even. Have people around that come from all walks of life, different backgrounds, different experiences, different traditions, cultures and different ways of thinking.

Reach out

Take the first step to launch new relationships. If you keep running into someone you'd like to know, suggest that you have lunch or coffee. Rather than saying, "your call", be specific and set a date. I always do this myself when I'm meeting with friends, or family, or people that I have become friends with over social media. When we want to meet up we'll arrange a specific date and a time, even when it comes to making a phone call because otherwise, in this day and age when people are so busy working, you won't get to see them. They'll always have other commitments, but with a date and time in their diary, they'll put time aside.

Many reputable social networking or other sites have forums to take you away from social media. You have forums that have conversations with other people, there are discussion groups, and blogs, personal online diaries for people with particular concerns, there's no end of great support out there. Another good way to find sites is to search online for a national organisation devoted to issues that may concern you maybe, something that you may be going through, or maybe even someone that you know close to you, and you need some extra advice and support.

Strong Network

Having a strong personal network can make your life easier while also showing you how much your support means to others. The best way to develop a network is to always give others as much as you hope to receive. I say hope to receive, it doesn't mean that you will, and that's okay It's more about giving without expecting anything back in return. If you do that, you won't be disappointed. You want to be able to give to people, share knowledge, share information, give advice the best way you can. That is one of the best feelings in the world and makes you feel so good. Especially when that person turns around and says, "Oh you know what? You've really helped me, thank you so much for your support, that's really helped me. You don't know what you've done for me."

On a serious note, and it could be the difference between someone going through a really, really dark place to actually almost bringing them out of it. I say this, not generalizing, but actually something that I've experienced with someone who I just happened to contact. It made that huge difference, so it does help. Don't expect any reciprocation. It doesn't have to be about someone giving you support or guidance back, it's just them just appreciating what you've done for them by saying, "thank you, I really appreciate your help. It's really helped me." I think that's definitely something that's quite huge, and rewarding.

There's a saying that goes, "The more you give, the more you receive." That will happen in time, and you'll start to see that. If you start to expect pretty much straight away, and feel let down every time you've helped someone and they haven't actually helped you back, apart from saying, "Thank you, I appreciate your support," you'll always be feeling let down.

That's something you need to come out of because you will find in time, because the more you give over time, you will receive, and you will receive, and you will receive. It will just be worth the wait, and definitely, good things come your way. That's the concept of having close relationships with family, friends, and networking in events, communities, and obviously online, social media, creating so many great friends who think alike. Obviously remembering to take out the negative people in your life so that you can make more room for the most positive like-minded people.

"Individually we are one drop, but together we are an ocean." — Ryunosuke Satoro

Chapter 8. GRATITUDE

Now I'm going to talk about the concept of gratitude. Some of you may already be aware or practice the art of gratitude every day. I'd like to start by saying its amazing how one simple, easy, positive action can change so much in a person's life.

One of the things that has had the biggest effect in my life, is the power of gratitude; simply giving thanks. It has affected everything. It has made me a more positive person, a more productive person, a better achiever, a better daughter, a better sister, a happier person.

No one, and I say this again, no one is perfect, but gratitude has made me a better person and it can make anyone better if you practice it. Can it change your life as well? Of course, I can guarantee it.

You might not get exactly the same benefits as I have but there's no doubt in my mind that the simple act of gratitude on a regular basis will change anyone's life positively and quite quickly. How many other changes can claim to be that quick, that easy and that profound? Going forward, let's look at some of the ways you can incorporate gratitude into your life and how it will change your life. These are just some examples based on my experiences. Not all will apply to your life but pick and choose and test the ones you think that will work for you.

Morning Gratitude Session

Take one minute in the morning and make it a daily ritual to think about the people who have done something nice for you. To think of all the things in your life that you're grateful for. You won't get to everything in one minute but it's enough and it will instantly make your day better and help you start your day off right. Can you think of a better use of one minute?

Make a Gratitude List

We all have those bad days; sometimes it's just the way it is. We get stressed out about work, we get yelled at by someone, we lose a loved one and we hurt a loved one. We lose a contract or do poorly on a project. It could be a number of reasons. One of the things that can make a bad day much better is making a list of all the things you're actually grateful for. There are always things to be grateful for. Loved ones, health, having a job, having a roof over your head and clothes on your back; being alive! I can tell you this but in my practice of gratitude it's not about the huge things, It's actually the small yet the necessary things in life to be grateful for, which in turn can bring you abundance.

Practice being grateful for the food you eat, the water you drink, the air you breathe, the people in your life, every day. Even the fact that you wake up every day and you open your eyes. There are many people out there, not quite as lucky, who weren't able to wake up this morning so be thankful for each day. Also, instead of getting mad at someone, show gratitude. There's a major switch in your attitudes, actually a complete flip. This isn't always easy to do, but I can promise you that is a great thing to do.

Expressing Gratitude towards Others

If you get mad at your co-worker for example because of something he or she said, bite your tongue and don't react in anger. Instead take some deep breaths, calm down and try and think of reasons you're grateful for that person. Has that person done anything nice for you? Has that person ever done a good job? Find something, anything, even if it's difficult. Focus on those things that make you grateful. It will slowly change your mood and if you get in a good enough mood, show your gratitude to that person. It will improve your mood, your relationship and help make things better. After showing gratitude, you can ask for a favour. "Can you please refrain from shredding my important documents in the future?" In the context of your gratitude, such a favour isn't such a hard thing for the co-worker to grant, so maybe you ought to think about that.

Instead of criticising your significant other, show gratitude. That is basically the same as the above tactic that I just mentioned but I wanted to point out how gratitude can transform a marriage or a relationship. If you constantly criticise you spouse, your marriage will slowly deteriorate, that I promise you. I'm not married but I can assure you by my experience of working with other people and also family and friends around me, I can say that. I can vouch and say those things.

It's important to be able to talk out problems but no one likes to be criticised all the time. Instead when you find yourself feeling the urge to criticise, stop and take a deep breath, calm down and think about all the reasons you're grateful for your spouse and share that gratitude as soon as possible. Your relationship will become stronger. Your spouse will learn from your example, especially if you do this all the time.

Embrace the Challenges

When you face a major challenge, be grateful for it. Many people will see something difficult as a bad thing. If something goes wrong, it's a reason to complain. It's a time for self-pity. That won't get you anywhere but I can tell you from my experiences, years of experiences in fact, instead learn to be grateful for the challenge. It's an opportunity to grow, to learn, to get better at something. This will transform you from a complainer into a positive person who only continues to improve. People will like you better and you'll improve your career.

Another really, really important one that sits closely to my heart, is when you suffer a tragedy. Be grateful for the life you still have. I mentioned this at the beginning of my book, about someone close to me who passed away years ago. Coming back to that, when I lost my dear uncle, it was crippling, I'm not saying you shouldn't grieve; of course you should. You can only take so much with such tragedies, however appreciation for life itself, love for the people who are still in your life, can help get you through. Take this opportunity to show appreciation to these people and to enjoy life while you can, because you don't know what tomorrow will bring.

Focus on What You Do Have

Last but not least, I'd say instead of looking at what you don't have, look at what you do have. Really important when practicing gratitude. Have you ever looked around you and bemoaned how little you have? How the place you live isn't your dream house or the car you drive isn't as nice as you'd like, or your peers have cooler things or better jobs than you? If so, this is an opportunity to be grateful for what you already have. It's easy to forget, but there are billions of people worse off than us who don't have much in the way of chattel or clothes, who don't own a car and don't have a job at all or only have very menial, miserable jobs and are working in certain dire conditions.

Compare your life to these people's lives and be grateful for the life you have. It's not about comparing yourself for your own gain to make yourself feel better or worse, it's about comparing your life to others and be grateful for the life you have, because there will always be someone worse off than you. They may not have much at all but it's ironic, it's those people who are happiest and smile the most if you think about it.

Those that have all the things in the world like cars, holidays, a beautiful house, family, everything, well deep inside they're still not happy because they're not grateful for what they already have. It's those people that have got less than us that always have smiles on their faces because they're grateful for what they have and realize that it's already more than enough. That happiness is not a destination it's actually already there here and now.

People often say (and I have done so too in the past), I'll be happy when I have the job, I'll be happy when I meet the partner, I'll be happy when I lose the weight, how about I'll be grateful for what I have right here, right now. Therefore the more grateful you are for what you have, that gets put out to the universe the more you will receive and it's the smallest things that count. Every day, if you write a list down of all the little things you're grateful for, see how each day that list grows and grows, and if it doesn't, by all means come back to me but I guarantee you it will grow.

I hope that has helped clarify things in terms of how to practice the art of gratitude. Whether it's getting a journal which already contains positive phrases and just writing in that or getting a plain notebook, you can do that. Below you will see I've also attached a couple of links of books that I think are absolutely incredible for practicing the art of gratitude, to you help you a little bit further.

VISUALISATION

If you struggle with visualisation, then I have some comforting news for you. You're normal. Sure there are some people who have the ability to close their eyes and instantly bring up crystal clear images, but for many of us this is a skill that needs to be developed over time. With practice however, everyone has the ability to visualize.

Visualisation of your goals and desires accomplishes four very important things:

1. **It activates your creative subconscious** which will start generating creative ideas to achieve your goal.
2. **It programs your brain** to more readily perceive and recognize the resources you will need to achieve your dreams.

3. **It activates the law of attraction**, thereby drawing into your life the people, resources, and circumstances you will need to achieve your goals.
4. **It builds your internal motivation** to take the necessary actions to achieve your dreams.

Visualisation is really quite simple. You sit in a comfortable position, close your eyes and imagine, in as vivid detail as you can, what you would be looking at if the dream you have were already realized. Imagine being inside of yourself, looking out through your eyes at the ideal result.

Practice Makes Perfect

There are two keys principles to keep in mind when practicing visualisation. The first is, that your practice needs to be consistent. 10 minutes a day every day, will always beat an intense hour long session once a week. It helps to make a commitment to practice your visualisation the same time every day. First thing in the morning as close to waking as possible is ideal. This is because the mind is still slightly lucid at this time, which makes it easier to conjure up images.

The second key principle is you need to stay positive. Even if you can't see crystal clear images yet, you will still gain huge benefits from your visualisation practice. It still works. Just connect to the image in whatever way you can. For some people that will be feeling the image or just getting a sense of what it might look like. Wherever your current level is, nurture it and allow it to grow.

Visualize What You Want

One of the most powerful effects of good visualization is that it programs the subconscious brain. You want to think of the subconscious brain as a self-guiding missile. When a self-guiding missile is fired, it starts moving towards its programmed target. As it moves towards its target it assesses its coordinates in relation to the target, and makes mini adjustments to correct its path. Our subconscious brain works in the same way. It identifies our coordinates and naturally moves us towards our target.

The problem with most people is that they program their subconscious mind with negative coordinates. They visualize images of failure, they replay mistakes, they think about negative scenarios that might happen, and picture the negative consequences that may arise. Unfortunately the subconscious mind doesn't judge. It doesn't say "those coordinates are negative so I'll just ignore them". In that way it's very similar to the GPS system in your car. The GPS doesn't judge, it simply takes you to the programmed destination. The theatre of your mind is the one place where you can ensure success. You can dominate your competition, and you can ensure victory. By visualizing success, you program your subconscious to move towards success.

Shift Perspective

Let's do a quick exercise. In a moment I'll ask you to close your eyes, and take your awareness to your breath. Trace the movement of the breath through your body. If possible follow it all the way to your belly, and then back up, releasing any tension as you go. With each breath you relax a little more. As you continue to relax, bring up an image of you in the sporting arena, competing. Where is this competition being held? Who are you competing against? See if you can involve all the senses. What do you see? What do you hear? What do you feel? Go a little deeper. What do you smell? Play around with this image of yourself. See yourself performing at your very best. Give yourself permission to dream, to push your current boundaries. Ok, so once you've done this and feel like you've really completely connected to this vision, read on.

Rev It up

The visualisation is important, but what's even more important is the feeling it creates inside of you. Visualisation without feeling is like a car without fuel. Feelings lead to emotions, and emotions are the fuel of your performance. Create powerful emotions, and you'll create powerful performance states. Based on this, a huge key to visualisation is pumping the experience, or in other words increasing the intensity of your emotions. There are a number of ways you can do this.

Here are a few books I've recommended in order to practise gratitude and the art of visualisation:

- *The Magic* — Rhonda Byrne
- *Choosing Gratitude* — Nancy Leigh DeMoss
- *Attitudes of Gratitude* — M. J. Ryan

"Feeling gratitude and not expressing it is like wrapping a present and not giving it." — William Arthur Ward

Chapter 9. SELF AWARENESS

Self-awareness is self-understanding and self-knowledge. It's getting to know your true, genuine self. It enables you to identify and understand factors of which you were NOT aware until now that control your reactions and behaviours and harm your relationships.

Being self-aware is a little like keeping a running inventory in your mind. Sure you need to know who you are as a whole person, but you also want to be aware of your strengths, weaknesses, and habits. You'll also want to know what you like and what you dislike, and what does and what doesn't motivate you. Your core values, those unwritten rules you live your life by, also need to be a part of your self-awareness inventory.

Above all, being self-aware means that you are able to live your life with self-confidence. You know who you are, what you want out of life and what you believe in. Because of this you're able to live life to the fullest each and every moment.

In order to become more self-aware, you need to know exactly who you are at this precise moment. These six tips will get you started on building your self-awareness and really learning who you are right now.

Figure out What Your Strong Points Are

Then go to work on listing the weakest ones too. Chances are that if you're like the majority of people, you have a tendency to focus on what you don't do well. Instead, start by concentrating on your strengths. Everyone has them, however minor they seem to you.

Yes, it's important to know your weaknesses too so that you know what areas need work, but don't sell your talents and your strengths short, expand on them and use them to create results you've always wanted.

Make an Inventory of Your Habits

You know you have them, whether you want to admit it or not. We all do and recognizing what they are and how they affect you on a daily basis is a great way of getting to know yourself.

Do you smoke? Are you a nail-biter? Are you always on time, or alternatively chronically late?

Again, make a list of all your good habits. Then make another list of what you would consider your bad habits. You'll be surprised at what these lists can reveal about you. The great thing is that bad habits are able to be changed. But you can't make the changes unless you have enough self-awareness to recognize them in the first place.

Make a List of the Things You Like and Dislike

This is the easy one. Knowing what you like and what you don't like is a very basic form of self-awareness. But have you ever taken the time to write it all down and admit that there are just some things that you'd really rather not spend your time doing? You may find that you spend a lot of time doing things you'd rather not because you don't want to let other people down. That's okay, but you also want to make sure that you spend time doing the things that speak to your heart too, now that you're more aware of what they are.

Having them written down on a list that stares you in the face works well too. It's a lot harder to ignore your likes when they're in plain view.

Know What Motivates You

Sometimes, you might have the desire to get something done, or to achieve a certain goal, but if the desire and ambition are not strong enough, you lack the push, the initiative, and the willingness to take the necessary action in these cases, you lack of motivation and inner drive.

Knowing what motivates you is an important part of becoming more self-aware. It's no secret that in order to live life to the fullest, we have to be able to motivate ourselves. If you lack motivation or don't have any, it will be extremely difficult to fulfill your dreams, this is why it is so important to know what gets you excited or makes you happy.

Motivation becomes strong, when you have a vision, a clear mental image of what you want to achieve, and also a strong desire to manifest it. In such a situation, motivation awakens inner strength and power, and pushes you forward, toward making your vision a reality.

Decide What Is Relevant to Your Life Right Now

This may seem like an easy decision but it's not quite as simple as it looks. Much of what we think we know about ourselves is based on past versions of ourselves. One of the things that

Geneen Roth writes about in the book "Women, Food and God" is that many of our ideas about who we are — our self-awareness — comes from outdated versions of ourselves. We make decisions based on fears of things that have happened in the past instead of on what is happening in our lives right now.

I say consider asking for feedback from people you trust, but only do this if you're comfortable with hearing things you'd maybe rather not. After all, you are building your own self-awareness and just by definition that's something that doesn't really take into account other people's opinions of you.

However, sometimes someone close to you can see patterns and habits that you might not be aware of. You can always add them to your list or accept or reject their insights as you see fit.

Chapter 10. AFFIRMATIONS

Simply stated, the purpose of affirmation is to pass a command from the conscious to the subconscious mind. The subconscious mind has the ability to accept anything it wants as true, to do whatever it takes to turn it into reality. The purpose of an affirmation is to pass a message to the subconscious mind, and to make it believe the message is true. So this brings us to the first element of an effective affirmation.

"Why don't my affirmations work?" "I can't remember to do my affirmations." "Oh why bother, I give up!" Do any of these sound familiar? Affirmations are powerful tools, but like any tools they need to be the right ones for the job and used in the right way. Here are some simple tips that can help you develop better affirmations.

Accentuate the Positive

The word affirmation comes from the verb affirm which means to state positively. When developing your affirmation statements, make sure they are in the positive. There is something about negative words that don't seem to register in our subconscious minds properly. The word 'not' in particular seems to cause the most trouble.

Here is a good example. Imagine that you are about to go on a first date with a very attractive partner. You've been looking forward to this and you say to yourself "I'm not going to mess up this date." Invariably what happens? You mess up the date somehow. These snafus are meant for sitcom episodes, not for manifesting your reality.

Remember to phrase your statements in the positive. For example if your affirmation is "I'm not going to get angry" try this instead "I remain calm." Positive statements bring a positive reality.

Present Tense

The universe technically has no past or future, everything is in the now. For this reason, keep your affirmations in the present tense. When you use a statement like "I remain calm" on a subconscious level you are saying that you already possess calmness. You may not really feel that way right now, but you need to "fake it until you make it" as the old saying goes. When you say "I will remain calm" you are basically telling the universe that you can wait until the future to manifest this request. Don't wait. You deserve to own your future now!

Short and Sweet

Simplicity is the key when wording your affirmations. You want something that is short and easy to remember. A lengthy phrase will be difficult to repeat and remember, thus tempting you to give up using it altogether. Write down your affirmation if you think it will help. Sometimes the act of writing and seeing it on paper makes it stick in your mind. Be sure to keep it brief!

Add Some Feeling

Affirmations are not much good if they are just words with no meaning behind them. Since you will be developing your own phrases rather than reading someone else's suggestions, you are already ahead of the game. The next thing to do is add an emotional component when you state your affirmations.

The best way to do this is to recall an event or time when you had a feeling of success and fulfilment. Relive that moment and those good feelings, before, during and after doing your affirmations. The idea is to transfer those positive emotions to your affirmations, giving them a boost. By doing this you are applying the law of attraction, using good vibrations experienced in the past to attract similar energy to manifest your desires.

Repeat, Repeat, Repeat

This tip seems pretty obvious, but it is much easier said than done. Consistency is very important for your affirmations to be successful. A good rule of thumb is to practice them at regular intervals, repeating them over and over.

Develop a routine. You may choose to devote ten minutes first thing in the morning, then again after dinner and before bed. You may also use an alarm or timer to remind you of your affirmation 'appointments' for the day. Do whatever works best for you, but make sure you do it!

Using these tips can immediately enhance your affirmations. You now have a good set of tools and a better way of using them. Soon these statements will sound familiar and you may say to yourself "wow, my affirmations are working well!" "I look forward to doing my affirmations." "This is great, I'll keep going!" Wishing you much success with your affirmations! Happy manifesting!

"Whatever the mind of man can conceive and believe, he can achieve." — Napoleon Hill

About the Author

Kam Bedi is a Personal Power Coach and Speaker who works with clients by asking them quality questions and prompting them to dig deeper within themselves. She has over 10 years of experience from dealing with people of all walks of life and a great understanding of how people think, behave and most importantly talk about themselves, which more often than not is negative, this is when the Personal Power Coach comes into play.

67628298R00059

Made in the USA
Charleston, SC
17 February 2017